Prélude

S. RACHMANINOFF. Op. 3, № 2

24087 x

4

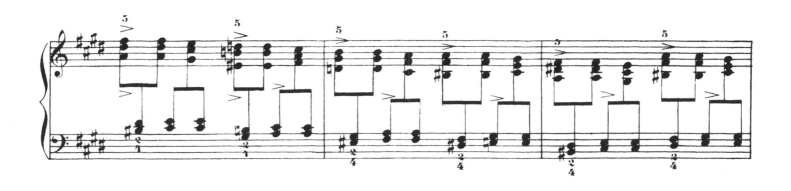

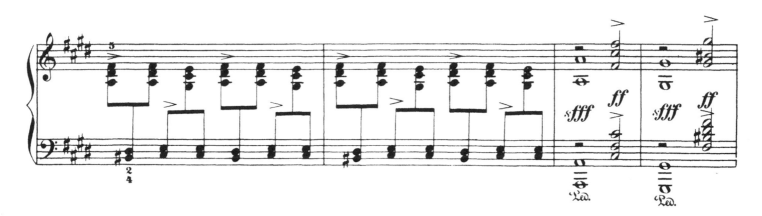

Tempo I

A Monsieur A. Arensky

Élégie

Edited and fingered by
Andor Pintér

S. Rachmaninoff. Op. 3, № 1

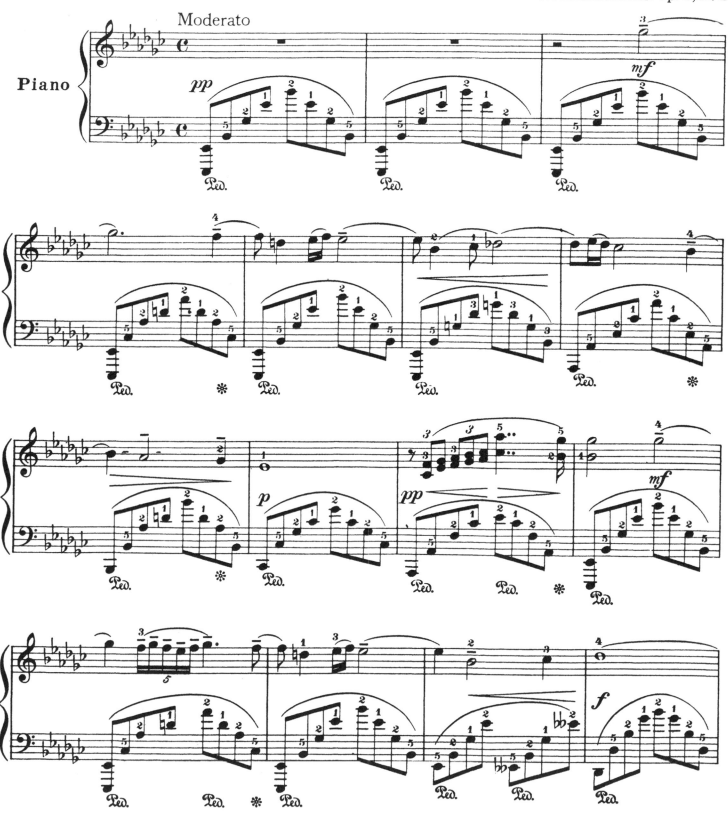

24037

9

24037

Più vivo

a tempo

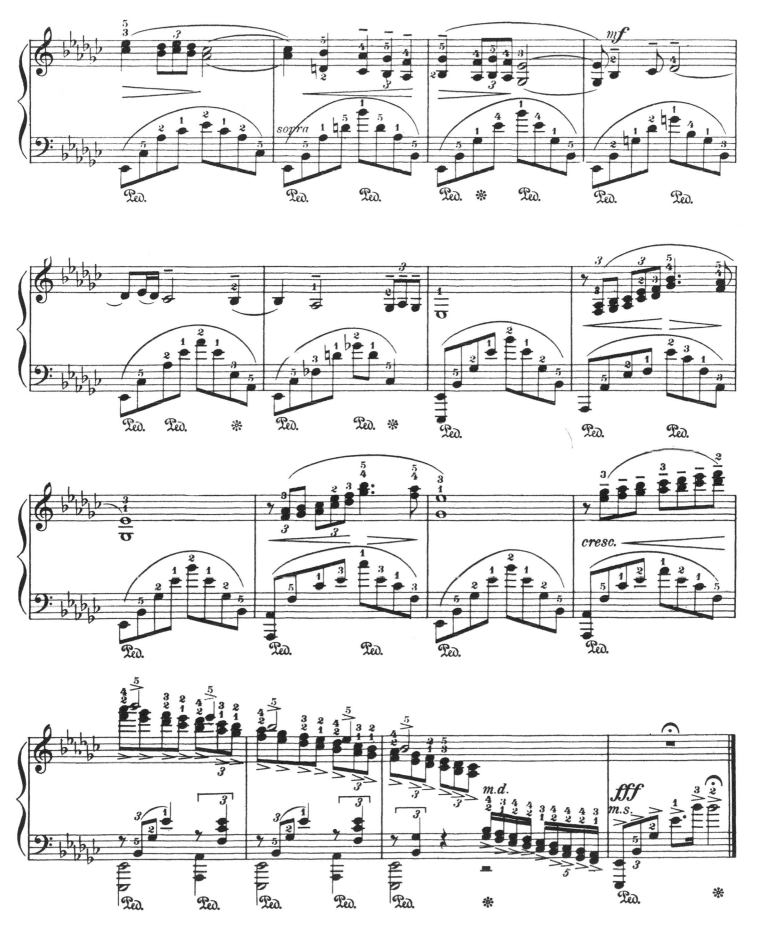

A Monsieur A. Arensky

Mélodie

Edited and fingered by
Andor Pintér

S. Rachmaninoff. Op. **3**, № **3**

Adagio sostenuto

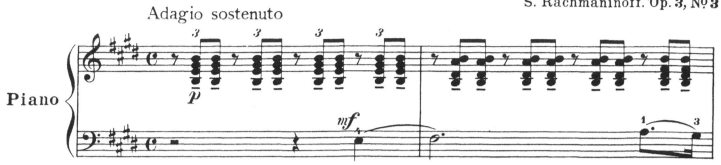

Piano

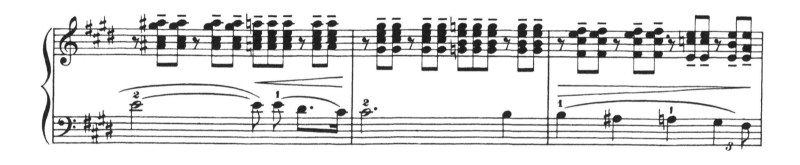

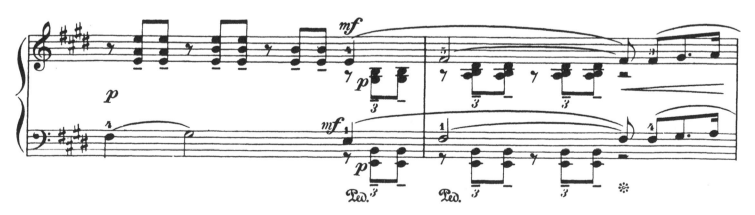

24037

24087

A Monsieur A. Arensky

Sérénade

Revised, with Fingering
and Pedal-marks, by
A. Siloti

S. Rachmaninoff. Op. 3

Tempo di Valse *(non troppo vivo)*

Valse

Edited and fingered by
Louis Oesterle

S. RACHMANINOFF. Op. 10, № 2

24087

24087

Allegro moderato

Polichinelle

Edited and fingered by
Louis Oesterle

S. RACHMANINOFF. Op. 3, № 4

Allegro vivace

Piano

84087

24037

Edited and fingered by
Louis Oesterle

A Monsieur A. Siloti

Prélude

S. Rachmaninoff. Op. 23, Nº 5

Piano

24037

Un. poco meno mosso

poco a poco accelerando e cresc. al Tempo I

Tempo I

Edited and fingered by
Louis Oesterle

A Monsieur Paul Pabst

Barcarolle

Moderato

S. Rachmaninoff. Op. 10, No 3

Piano

24037

Con moto

24087

Second Piano Concerto
Third Movement

Sergei Rachmaninoff, Op. 18
Condensed and arranged by
Carl Deis

24037

quasi glissando

Maestoso ♩ = 60